The North Carolina Tar Heels™

BY
MARK STEWART

Content Consultant
Matt Zeysing
Historian and Archivist
The Naismith Memorial Basketball Hall of Fame

NORWOOD HOUSE PRESS
CHICAGO, ILLINOIS

Norwood House Press
P.O. Box 316598
Chicago, Illinois 60631

For information regarding Norwood House Press, please visit our website at:
www.norwoodhousepress.com or call 866-565-2900.

All photos courtesy of Getty Images except the following:
Associated Press (15, 18, 31, 37 bottom), University of North Carolina (10, 12, 26, 32, 39),
Collegiate Collection (6, 29, 33, 36 left, 41 top), Author's Collection (7, 28, 40, 41 bottom),
Condé Nast Publications (14), Courtside, Inc. (17, 36 right), Basketball Times (21),
Classic Games/Sprint (23), Editions Rencontre, S.A. (24), Student Sports Publishing (25),
Pinnacle Brands, Inc. (37 top left), TIME Inc./Sports Illustrated (37 top right), Matt Richman (48).
Cover Photo: Gregory Shamus/Getty Images

Special thanks to Topps, Inc.

Editor: Mike Kennedy
Designer: Ron Jaffe
Project Management: Black Book Partners, LLC.
Editorial Production: Jessica McCulloch
Research: Joshua Zaffos
Special thanks to Kathryn Roth and Jessica Thompson

Library of Congress Cataloging-in-Publication Data

Stewart, Mark, 1960-
  The North Carolina Tar Heels / by Mark Stewart.
     p. cm. -- (Team spirit--college basketball)
  Includes bibliographical references and index.
  Summary: "Presents the history and accomplishments of the University of
North Carolina Tar Heels basketball team. Includes highlights of players,
coaches, and awards, longstanding rivalries, quotes, timeline, maps,
glossary, and websites"--Provided by publisher.
   ISBN-13: 978-1-59953-366-7 (library edition : alk. paper)
   ISBN-10: 1-59953-366-9 (library edition : alk. paper)
  1. University of North Carolina at Chapel
Hill--Basketball--History--Juvenile literature. 2. North Carolina Tar Heels
(Basketball team)--History--Juvenile literature. I. Title.
   GV885.43.U54S74 2010
   796.323'6309756565--dc22
                                                          2009033809

Manufactured in the United States of America in North Mankato, Minnesota.
159N—072010

COVER PHOTO: The Tar Heels rush the court after their 2009 national championship.

Table of Contents

SPORTS WORDS & VOCABULARY WORDS: In this book, you will find many words that are new to you. You may also see familiar words used in new ways. The glossary on page 46 gives the meanings of basketball words, as well as "everyday" words that have special basketball meanings. These words appear in **bold type** throughout the book. The glossary on page 47 gives the meanings of vocabulary words that are not related to basketball. They appear in ***bold italic type*** throughout the book.

Meet the Tar Heels

The mark of a great college basketball team is consistency. Playing well and winning games—year in and year out—is difficult when players come and go every season. The keys are good team *tradition*, a talented coach, and loyal fans. Those are just some of the things that make the University of North Carolina (UNC) one of the top teams in the nation.

Something else that makes the Tar Heels successful is their history. For UNC players, signs of the team's proud past are everywhere. The championship banners tell the story—the team's 2009 national title was the fifth for the school. The names of the players who have worn the Carolina uniform read like a "Who's Who" of college basketball.

This book tells the story of the Tar Heels. For UNC and its fans, every year starts as a championship season. The sky's the limit at the Chapel Hill *campus*, and the color of that sky is Carolina blue.

Marvin Williams jumps into the arms of Sean May after North Carolina's 2005 national championship.

Way Back When

NORTH CAROLINA'S FINEST

CARTWRIGHT CARMICHAEL

Basketball has been a way of life at North Carolina for a *century*. The school's first team took the court in 1910. That season, UNC won its first game, against Virginia Christian, 42–21. For more than 30 seasons, Carolina was a member of the **Southern Conference**. The team was conference champion eight times.

The school enjoyed its first great season in 1923–24. That team was led by Jack Cobb, Bill Dodderer, and Cartwright Carmichael. In those days, UNC was called the "Blue and White" (and also the "White Phantoms"). Carolina won all 22 of its games during the regular season, and then beat Kentucky, Vanderbilt, Mississippi State, and Alabama to take the Southern Conference Tournament. The **National Collegiate Athletic Association (NCAA)** did not hold a tournament at that time, but UNC was later named the national champion.

Carolina left the Southern Conference in 1953 to help form the new **Atlantic Coast Conference (ACC)**. The team was now known as the Tar Heels, and soon they became a basketball powerhouse. Coach Frank McGuire **recruited** top players from New York City. His

"Carolina Yankees" included Lennie Rosenbluth and Tommy Kearns. In 1956–57, they led the team to another undefeated season and a second national championship.

Four years later, McGuire's young assistant, Dean Smith, replaced him as the team's coach. In college games, mistakes often are the difference between winning and losing. Smith made sure his Tar Heels mastered the basics of basketball. That made Carolina very difficult to beat.

During the 1960s and 1970s, UNC seemed to have a star-filled **lineup** every year. The school's **All-ACC** guards included Larry Brown, Bob Lewis, Charlie Scott, Phil Ford, and Walter Davis. The Tar Heels also had plenty of star power along the front line, including forwards Billy Cunningham, Larry Miller, Bobby Jones, and Mike O'Koren. UNC's best big men during this era were Bob McAdoo and Mitch Kupchak. Carolina reached the **Final Four** each year

LEFT: A trading card of Cartwright Carmichael.
ABOVE: A signed photo of Larry Brown.

from 1967 to 1969 and two more times during the 1970s. But Smith could never quite lead his team to the national title.

In 1981, the Tar Heels reached the championship game, but they lost to Indiana. That team starred Al Wood, James Worthy, Sam Perkins, Matt Doherty, and Jimmy Black. They were fine players, but something was missing. The following season, a teenager named Michael Jordan joined the team. He turned out to be the final piece of the puzzle. Jordan gained experience as the 1981–82 season wore on. At the end of the year, he made the shot that gave Smith his long-awaited national championship.

More great stars joined the Tar Heels in the years that followed. Brad Daugherty, Kenny Smith, and J.R. Reid were among the top players in the country. In the early 1990s, the Tar Heels built another championship team. It featured George Lynch, Donald Williams, and Eric Montross. Carolina defeated Michigan in the 1993 **NCAA Tournament** final for Smith's second championship.

Smith retired in 1997 with more victories than any coach in the history of **Division I** basketball. His longtime assistant, Bill Guthridge, coached the team for three seasons. He reached the Final Four twice with the help of Antawn Jamison, Vince Carter, Brendan Haywood, Ademola Okulaja, and Joe Forte. To return to championship form, however, Carolina would look to a new leader.

Dean Smith gives instructions to Michael Jordan during the 1981–82 season.

21st Century

In the early years of the 21st century, the Tar Heels found themselves in an unfamiliar place—at the bottom of the ACC **standings**. Carolina struggled to put a winning team on the floor for the first time in more than 30 years. In 2001–02, UNC was not invited to compete in the NCAA Tournament. That hadn't happened since the 1970s!

Luckily, the school's winning tradition convinced young high school stars that the team would soon be back on top. The Tar Heels quickly rebuilt under new coach Roy Williams. He relied on excellent players like Sean May, Rashad McCants, Raymond Felton, Marvin Williams, Wayne Ellington, Tyler Hansbrough, and Ty Lawson. UNC returned to the top of college basketball. Coach Williams guided Carolina to the national title in 2005 and 2009.

UNC's basketball "machine" is running more smoothly than ever. As the team's top players graduate or move on to play in the **National Basketball Association (NBA)**, new stars are ready to replace them. Each season, fans can hardly wait to see who will step forward to keep the Tar Heels among the *elite* teams in college sports.

Roy Williams hugs Ty Lawson after North Carolina's victory in the 2009 championship game.

Home Court

The Tar Heels have called three arenas home over the last 70 years. Their home court during their 1956–57 championship season was the Woollen Gymnasium. In 1965, Carmichael Auditorium was built right next door. In fact, it shared a wall with Woollen. Carmichael was one of the noisiest arenas in the United States, thanks to a low ceiling and loud fans.

In 1986, the Tar Heels moved into the new Dean Smith Center—or the "Dean Dome," as students call it. The Dean Dome is one of the largest basketball arenas in the country. It sells out every game. This gives the Tar Heels a great advantage. In fact, fans are surprised and disappointed if Carolina loses more than one or two games a year at home.

BY THE NUMBERS

- *The Dean Dome has 21,750 seats for basketball.*
- *The arena cost $33 million to build in 1986.*
- *As of 2009, the visiting Clemson Tigers had not won a game at the Dean Dome in 24 tries.*

The Dean Dome is usually a sea of Carolina blue on game day.

Dressed for Success

The main colors of the UNC uniform are white and Carolina blue. They remind fans of the state's warm skies and date back more than a century. In the early 1800s, students at the school dressed in light blue or white, depending on which campus society (or club) they belonged to. When UNC started competing in athletics, both colors were used in the uniforms.

The basketball team wears white with blue lettering at home and blue with white lettering on the road. The uniforms spell out the name of the state. The Tar Heels have also used an interlocking *N-C **logo*** on their uniforms.

What is a Tar Heel? It is an old nickname given to North Carolinians. There are many stories about how it started. Most people like to think it came from the Civil War, when the state's soldiers were known for standing and fighting against great odds—as if they had sticky tar on their heels.

Tommy Kearns models the Carolina uniform from the 1950s.

UNIFORM BASICS

The basketball uniform is very simple. It consists of a roomy top and baggy shorts.

- The top hangs from the shoulders, with big "scoops" for the arms and neck. This style has not changed much over the years.

- Shorts, however, have changed a lot. They used to be very short, so players could move their legs freely. In the last 20 years, shorts have gotten longer and much baggier.

Basketball uniforms look the same as they did long ago … until you look very closely. In the old days, the shorts had belts and buckles. The tops were made of a thick cotton called "jersey," which got very heavy when players sweated. Later, uniforms were made of shiny **satin**. They may have looked great, but they did not "breathe." As a result, players got very hot! Today, most uniforms are made of **synthetic** materials that soak up sweat and keep the body cool.

Danny Green celebrates a good play wearing the team's 2008–09 home uniform.

We're Number 1!

From 1957 to 2009, the Tar Heels won the NCAA Tournament five times. Coach Frank McGuire built their first championship team around five starters from the playgrounds of New York City—Lennie Rosenbluth, Tommy Kearns, Pete Brennan, Bobby Cunningham, and Joe Quigg.

In the semifinal game against Michigan State, the Tar Heels needed three **overtimes** to win. The following day, they had to play Kansas and its superstar, Wilt Chamberlain. McGuire knew he had to do something to shake up the confident Jayhawks and loosen up his own players. He sent Kearns—the smallest of his starters—to take the opening jump ball against Chamberlain. After that, McGuire ordered the Tar Heels to triple-team the giant center and leave two Kansas players wide open. The crafty coach was betting that the Jayhawks would not be used to taking shots without a defender in front of them. He was right.

Carolina built a lead in an entertaining first half. The Jayhawks came back and moved ahead in the second half. Then Kansas decided to slow the game down, hoping to protect its lead. There was no **shot clock** back then, so a team could hold the ball as long as it wanted.

Sam Perkins could score with either hand. This card shows him shooting left-handed.

The **strategy** backfired. The Carolina players caught their breath and tied the game. They won 54–53 in triple-overtime—their second long game in two days!

Carolina's next title came in 1982. After losing the championship game in 1968, 1977, and 1981, coach Dean Smith was beginning to wonder if his team would ever win it all. The answer came in the form of freshman Michael Jordan. There was nothing "MJ" couldn't do. He teamed with Sam Perkins and James Worthy to lead the Tar Heels back to the title game.

Carolina's opponent, Georgetown, had a scary team. Eric "Sleepy" Floyd scored points in bunches. Freshman center Patrick Ewing played defense like a tornado. The two teams battled back and forth all game. Neither could gain control. Floyd made an amazing, off-balance shot to put Georgetown ahead 62–61. But Jordan had the last laugh. He hit a 16-foot jumper to give the Tar Heels a 63–62 victory.

Smith's second championship came in 1993. It shocked a lot of Carolina fans—and probably surprised Smith himself. Team leaders

Eric Montross, Derrick Phelps, and George Lynch were good players, but no one considered them stars. The key for Carolina was its great defense. When the NCAA Tournament started, sophomore Donald Williams got hot. In the semifinal against Kansas, he hit five **3-pointers** in a 78–68 victory.

In the championship game, Carolina beat Michigan, 77–71. Williams continued his excellent shooting, but the contest was close right to the end. In the final minutes, UNC's stubborn defense made the difference, forcing the young Wolverines into critical errors. The last one was committed by Michigan's Chris Webber with just a few seconds left on the clock.

Roy Williams coached the Tar Heels to their next championships, in 2005 and 2009. The 2004–05 squad was one of the school's best ever. It starred Sean May, Rashad McCants, Raymond Felton, and

Marvin Williams. The Tar Heels blew opponents off the court, including in the semifinal game, when they scored 54 points in the second half against Michigan State. UNC continued its fine play in the final against Illinois, winning 75–70. May was named the **Most Outstanding Player (MOP)** for his scoring and rebounding.

Coach Williams had to rebuild after all of his top scorers left Carolina for the NBA. By 2008–2009, he had assembled another excellent team. His leaders were senior Tyler Hansbrough and junior Ty Lawson. UNC's national championship that season might have been the school's greatest.

The Tar Heels won six games from the first round to the last game, and none of those victories were ever in doubt. In fact, Carolina outscored its opponents by more than 20 points a contest. Against Michigan State in the final, UNC raced out to a huge lead. The game was all but over in the first half. The final score was 89–72. Wayne Ellington was named the tournament's MOP.

LEFT: Carolina's tough defense swarms around Chris Webber in the final seconds of the 1993 championship game.   **ABOVE**: Wayne Ellington and Deon Thompson jump for joy after UNC's 2009 national title.

Go-To Guys

TROPHY CASE
These Tar Heels have won major awards.

GEORGE GLAMACK   6′ 7″ Center

• BORN: 6/7/1919   • DIED: 3/10/1987   • PLAYED FOR VARSITY: 1938–39 TO 1940–41

George Glamack was the best player in the nation in the early 1940s. He was named an **All-American** and the Player of the Year in 1940 and 1941. Glamack's 45 points against Clemson is still one of the highest single-game scoring totals in school history.

JAMES WORTHY   6′ 9″ Forward

• BORN: 2/27/1961   • PLAYED FOR VARSITY: 1979–80 TO 1981–82

James Worthy was a quick and clever forward who starred in UNC's fast-paced offense. He led the team in scoring during the 1981–82 championship season and was named the MOP in the NCAA Tournament. Worthy was the first pick in the 1982 NBA **draft**.

MICHAEL JORDAN   6′ 6″ Guard

• BORN: 2/17/1963   • PLAYED FOR VARSITY: 1981–82 TO 1983–84

Although Michael Jordan had great individual skills, he fit perfectly into Dean Smith's team-oriented system. He was the ACC's top freshman in 1981–82 and made the shot that won the NCAA championship that season. In 1983–84, Jordan won the Naismith Award and the Wooden Award, both as the top college player.

ANTAWN JAMISON   6′ 9″ Forward

• BORN: 6/12/1976   • PLAYED FOR VARSITY: 1995–96 TO 1997–98

On any given day, the Tar Heels could count on Antawn Jamison to give them 20 points and 10 rebounds. When the team needed a big basket, he always seemed to have the ball in his hands. Jamison won the Naismith and Wooden awards in 1997–98.

TYLER HANSBROUGH   6′ 9″ Forward

• BORN: 11/3/1985

• PLAYED FOR VARSITY: 2005–06 TO 2008–09

Tyler Hansbrough was a top scorer and defensive player from the moment he joined the Tar Heels. He was named All-ACC in each of his four seasons and set a conference record for the most 20-point games in a career. Hansbrough won the Naismith and Wooden awards as a junior in 2007–08.

Tyler Hansbrough

TY LAWSON   5′ 11″ Guard

• BORN: 11/3/1987

• PLAYED FOR VARSITY: 2006–07 TO 2008–09

Ty Lawson almost left Carolina for the NBA in 2008. UNC fans are glad he changed his mind. Lawson was named 2009 ACC Player of the Year and led the team to the national title. His eight steals in the championship game against Michigan State set an NCAA record.

SUPER SCORERS

These Tar Heels were hard to stop when they shot the basketball.

LENNIE ROSENBLUTH   6′ 5″ Forward

• BORN: 1/22/1933   • PLAYED FOR VARSITY: 1954–55 TO 1956–57

Lennie Rosenbluth used his quickness and shooting ability to average more than 25 points a game in each of his varsity seasons. More than 50 years after he scored 895 points as a senior, Rosenbluth still holds the school record for a single season.

BILLY CUNNINGHAM   6′ 6″ Forward

• BORN: 6/3/1943   • PLAYED FOR VARSITY: 1962–63 TO 1964–65

No one in the ACC could outjump or outscore Billy Cunningham. He set school records with 27 rebounds in a 1963 game against Clemson and 48 points against Tulane in 1964. The "Kangaroo Kid" averaged 24.8 points and 15.4 rebounds a game with UNC and was the team's **Most Valuable Player (MVP)** in each of his three seasons.

LARRY MILLER   6′ 4″ Forward

• BORN: 4/4/1946

• PLAYED FOR VARSITY: 1965–66 TO 1967–68

Larry Miller was the ACC Player of the Year twice as a Tar Heel. When he got hot, nobody could stop him. Miller led the team to the Final Four twice and averaged more than 21 points a game at UNC. Later, as a **professional**, Miller scored 67 points in a game.

22

CHARLIE SCOTT   6′ 5″ Guard

• BORN: 12/15/1948   • PLAYED FOR VARSITY: 1967–68 TO 1969–70

Charlie Scott was the first African-American athlete to receive a scholarship at North Carolina. He earned every bit of it. After his first season, Scott was picked for the **Olympic** team. He helped Team USA win a gold medal.

WALTER DAVIS   6′ 6″ Forward

• BORN: 9/9/1954   • PLAYED FOR VARSITY: 1973–74 TO 1976–77

Walter Davis was such a fun scorer to watch that teammates called him "Sweet D" and "Candy Man." He used his speed and instincts to get open shots whenever he wanted them. Davis was just as comfortable taking a long jump shot as he was driving to the basket for a layup.

JERRY STACKHOUSE   6′ 6″ Forward

• BORN: 11/5/1974

• PLAYED FOR VARSITY: 1993–94 TO 1994–95

Jerry Stackhouse played only two years in Chapel Hill before jumping to the NBA, but they were both great seasons. As a freshman, he was named MVP of the ACC Tournament. As a sophomore, Stackhouse led the Tar Heels in scoring and in steals.

LEFT: Billy Cunningham
ABOVE: Jerry Stackhouse

GAME CHANGERS

These Tar Heels had a special talent for controlling the flow of a game.

LARRY BROWN   5′ 9″ Guard

• Born: 9/14/1940   • Played for Varsity: 1960–61 to 1962–63

Larry Brown was Dean Smith's first star. Brown was an excellent ball

Basketball
The Four-corner Offense

handler and passer. He was also a tough *competitor*. When the Tar Heels needed a basket—or had to prevent one—Brown was usually involved in the play.

PHIL FORD   6′ 2″ Guard

• Born: 2/9/1956

• Played for Varsity: 1974–75 to 1977–78

Phil Ford was the best player in the ACC for most of his college career—and the top player in the country as a senior. No one ran coach Smith's **Four Corners offense** better than Ford. He later became an assistant coach for the Tar Heels.

BOBBY JONES   6′ 9″ Forward

• Born: 12/18/1951   • Played for Varsity: 1971–72 to 1973–74

When Bobby Jones arrived at Chapel Hill, he already did the things that make coaches smile. He positioned himself perfectly on defense, boxed out opponents on rebounds, and dove for **loose balls**. Jones also loved to finish Carolina's **fast break** with thunderous dunks.

BRAD DAUGHERTY 7′ 0″ Center

• BORN: 10/19/1965 • PLAYED FOR VARSITY: 1982–83 TO 1985–86

When Brad Daugherty wanted to score, no one in the ACC could stop him. But the *agile* center was more than just a scorer—he passed, rebounded, and played good defense. Daugherty made more than 60 percent of his shots as a Tar Heel. He led the ACC in scoring and rebounding in his senior year.

KENNY SMITH 6′ 3″ Guard

• BORN: 3/8/1965 • PLAYED FOR VARSITY: 1983–84 TO 1986–87

With Kenny Smith playing point guard, the Tar Heels went undefeated in the ACC during his freshman and senior seasons. His nickname was the "Jet" because of his amazing speed. When Smith graduated, he held the record for most **assists** in NCAA Tournament history.

VINCE CARTER 6′ 6″ Guard/Forward

• BORN: 1/26/1977

• PLAYED FOR VARSITY: 1995–96 TO 1997–98

What do you do when a player can jump right over you for layups, dunks, and 3-pointers? You get out of the way and hope he misses! For three seasons, that is what Carolina's opponents did when Vince Carter had the ball. Carter was the most exciting player in the ACC during the 1990s.

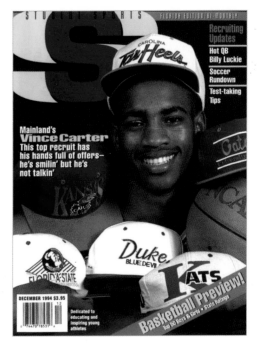

LEFT: During the 1970s, Phil Ford was the master of the Four Corners offense. **ABOVE**: As this magazine shows, Vince Carter had his pick of colleges—and chose UNC.

On the Sidelines

In 1923–24, Carolina featured a lineup of excellent shooters and smart players. But UNC became a championship squad that season because of coach Norman Shepard. He understood the game and knew how to blend the talents of his stars.

The team's next great coach was Frank McGuire. His players were confident that he could come up with a winning game plan, no matter who the opponent was. When McGuire left UNC, he recommended assistant Dean Smith to replace him. Smith saw that the sport was changing quickly and becoming more athletic. He also understood the importance of good basketball *fundamentals*.

Smith demanded that the Tar Heels play **team basketball**. This often made the difference between winning and losing. When Smith retired in 1997, he had taken Carolina to the Final Four 11 times, won two NCAA titles, and had 879 wins—more than anyone in Division I history. Smith's former players and assistants learned well from him. Bill Guthridge, Matt Doherty, and Roy Williams were all named Coach of the Year for UNC. Williams led the Tar Heels to the national championship in 2005 and 2009.

Dean Smith, considered by many the greatest coach in Carolina history.

Rivals

The campuses of North Carolina and Duke are just a few minutes apart. The students eat at the same restaurants, shop at the same stores, and go to the same concerts. They are polite and friendly to one another. But when the Tar Heels meet the Blue Devils on the basketball court, all of these things are forgotten.

UNC and Duke have one of the greatest *rivalries* ever.

The rivalry first heated up in 1960–61 when Larry Brown got into a fight with Duke star Art Heyman. Tensions continued to build in the late 1970s, when both schools were among the best in the country. The rivalry got more interesting after Mike Krzyzewski became Duke's coach. He was one of the few men who could match wits with Dean Smith.

Today when the schools meet, it is one of the biggest events in all of sports—not just college basketball. In March of 2006, Carolina beat the top-ranked Blue Devils on their home court. Nearly four million TVs around the U.S. were tuned into the game!

LEFT: This pennant says it all about the Carolina–Duke rivalry.
RIGHT: A trading card of 1959 hero York Larese.

NORTH CAROLINA'S FINEST

YORK LARESE

There have been many *unforgettable* moments for the Tar Heels in their games against Duke. In 1974, the teams were tied with just a few seconds left. Duke set up a play to win the game, but Bobby Jones stole the ball and raced down the court. He made a layup just before time ran out for a 73–71 victory.

Four years later, Phil Ford torched Duke for 34 points to give Carolina the ACC championship. It was the last regular-season home game of Ford's career, and he gave UNC fans a wonderful "good-bye" present.

The rivalry with Duke has turned many Tar Heels into heroes. The names of players like York Larese are still alive on the Chapel Hill campus. In a 1959 game against the Blue Devils, he made all 21 of his free throws to lead Carolina to victory. The roughness of the rivalry has also given fans some memorable pictures. No Carolina fan will ever forget the images of Eric Montross and Tyler Hansbrough, whose faces were bloodied in great battles with the Blue Devils.

One Great Day

By the time the Tar Heels battled their way to the 1982 NCAA championship game, most fans knew there was something special about young Michael Jordan. Coach Dean Smith's "team first" system did not allow the freshman to show off all his skills. Still, every so often, Jordan would make an amazing shot or spectacular dunk. Older teammates would just shake their heads in awe.

But as UNC prepared to meet Georgetown for the national title, no one was talking about Jordan. All the attention was on opposing center Patrick Ewing. The Hoyas had tough, smart players who used a **zone defense** to "funnel" their opponents toward Ewing. He would then swat their shots away.

Early in the championship game, Ewing was *dominating* near the basket. Georgetown seemed ready to take control. But Smith adjusted his offense, and soon the contest was tied. The teams traded baskets the rest of the way. Near the end of the second half, James Worthy dunked the ball to give Carolina the lead. But Sleepy Floyd responded to put the Hoyas ahead 62–61 with less than a minute left.

Dean Smith and the Tar Heels celebrate as Michael Jordan heads down the court after his game-winning shot against Georgetown.

Coach Smith called timeout and sketched out a play. He knew the Hoyas would expect Worthy to get the ball. Smith thought Jordan would be open. Sure enough, when guard Jimmy Black whipped a pass across the court to Jordan, the freshman was all alone. Jordan swished a shot to put Carolina ahead 63–62. Later he admitted that he closed his eyes as the ball neared the rim—he was too nervous to watch his own shot!

The Hoyas rushed down the court with the ball. Fred Brown heard a teammate call for a pass. Without thinking, he threw the ball right to Worthy. The Hoyas immediately fouled him. Carolina fans squirmed in their seats as he missed both free throws. However, Georgetown did not have enough time to take another shot, and the championship belonged to the Tar Heels.

It Really Happened

asketball fans can argue endlessly about which Carolina–Duke game was the best ever. There have been some great ones. The wildest may have been the final game of the 1973–74 season. Carolina was led by Bobby Jones and Walter Davis. The Blue Devils were not having a good year, but they always played like champions against the Tar Heels.

Duke was fantastic on this day. Playing on Carolina's home court, the Blue Devils led by eight points with just 17 seconds left. Some fans gave up and left their seats. They would regret that decision for the rest of their lives!

Jones drew a foul and hit two free throws to make the score 86–

LEFT: Bobby Jones leaps high to block a shot in a game against Duke. His great defense helped the Tar Heels stun the Blue Devils in the final game of the 1973–74 regular season. **RIGHT**: A trading card of Walter Davis—his 30-foot shot tied the game at the buzzer.

NORTH CAROLINA'S FINEST

WALTER DAVIS

80. Duke committed a **turnover**, and Carolina quickly scored again. The Tar Heels went to a **full-court press**, and the Blue Devils panicked. Jones stole a pass and made a layup with six seconds to go. The score was now 86–84.

Duke got the ball in to Pete Kramer. Carolina fouled him on purpose with four seconds left. Kramer missed his first free throw. The Tar Heels grabbed the rebound and called timeout. There were now three seconds left, and the fans were going crazy.

Dean Smith called a play for Davis. He got the ball, took two dribbles, and fired a 30-footer. The ball banked into the basket for two points at the buzzer to knot the score at 86–86.

The Tar Heels took care of business in the overtime period. They outscored Duke 10–6 to win 96–92. Davis finished with 31 points, and his bomb at the buzzer went down in college basketball history as one of the greatest shots of all time.

Team Spirit

UNC's *mascot* is Rameses, a feisty ram who loves to bang heads with opponents. He has been around since the 1920s. Carolina got its mascot thanks to a cheerleader named Vic Huggins. He believed the school's sports teams needed a tough nickname, like the Georgia Bulldogs and the North Carolina State Wolfpack. The star of UNC's football team at the time was Jack "Battering Ram" Merritt. That sounded like a good nickname to Huggins. He raised some money and ordered a live ram from Texas. A great tradition was born!

Bringing a live ram to indoor basketball games was a little different than leading him onto a grassy football field. In time, the Tar Heels decided that Rameses should be a student in a mascot costume. Over the years, it became a great honor to play Rameses at UNC games.

In 2007, Carolina students and families were heartbroken when they heard that Jason Ray, the young man who was to dress up as Rameses for an NCAA Tournament game, was killed in a traffic accident. Since then, the Jason Ray Memorial Spirit Award has been given to a member of the band, cheerleading squad, dance team, or a mascot performer who excels in the classroom and community.

Rameses gets a ride from excited Carolina fans.

Timeline

The basketball season is played from October through March. That means each season takes place at the end of one year and the beginning of the next. In this timeline, the accomplishments of the team are shown by season.

1923–24
Carolina is named national champion.

1956–57
The Tar Heels are national champions again.

1910–11
The Tar Heels play their first game.

1968–69
Carolina reaches the Final Four for the third year in a row.

1975–76
Mitch Kupchak is ACC Player of the Year.

Bob Lewis, a star for Carolina in the 1960s.

Dean Smith, the coach of the 1968–69 team.

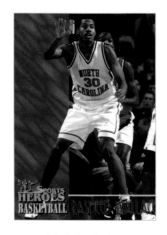

Rasheed Wallace

Tyler Hansbrough, who made the 2009 Tar Heels front-page news.

1994–95
Jerry Stackhouse and Rasheed Wallace are named to the All-ACC team.

2008–09
The Tar Heels win their fifth national championship.

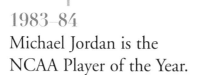

1983–84
Michael Jordan is the NCAA Player of the Year.

2003–04
Roy Williams becomes UNC's coach.

2009–10
The Tar Heels win their 2,000th game.

Roy Williams gives instructions to Raymond Felton.

Fun Facts

OH SAY, CAN YOU SEE?

George Glamack had a great shot but poor eyesight. His nickname was the "Blind Bomber." Glamack used the lines on the court to help him aim his shot. He led the Tar Heels in scoring during the 1940s.

STAT MASTER

In 2000, Ed Cota became the first player in school history with 1,000 points, 1,000 assists, and 500 rebounds in his college career.

FOREIGN SERVICE

In 1992–93, Henrik Rödl became the first German player to win a national championship. Dean Smith had discovered Rödl playing for nearby Chapel Hill High School as an exchange student in the 1980s.

BLOCK PARTY

Brendan Haywood was a one-man "SWAT Team" for the Tar Heels. He set school records for blocked shots with 10 in a game, 120 in a season, and 304 for his career.

Brad Daugherty dunks for an easy two points.

HOT SHOTS

In 1985, Brad Daugherty made 13 shots in a row during a game against UCLA. In 1989, Jeff Lebo set a school record when he made 41 free throws in a row. During the 2004–05 season, Raymond Felton made 12 consecutive 3-pointers.

DEAN DRAMA

In 1965, Carolina students demanded that the team hire a new coach. The Tar Heels had just lost four games in a row, which led to a campus protest. The school decided to give their young coach another chance. His name was Dean Smith.

NOTHING BUT NET

In 1995, Shammond Williams and Vince Carter became the first two college athletes to have their own web sites.

For the Record

The great North Carolina teams, coaches, and players have left their marks on the record books. These are the "best of the best" …

TAR HEELS AWARD WINNERS

HELMS FOUNDATION PLAYER OF THE YEAR

Jack Cobb	1925–26
George Glamack	1939–40
George Glamack	1940–41
Lennie Rosenbluth	1956–57

WOODEN AWARD

Phil Ford	1977–78
Michael Jordan	1983–84
Antawn Jamison	1997–98
Tyler Hansbrough	2007–08

NAISMITH AWARD

Michael Jordan	1983–84
Antawn Jamison	1997–98
Tyler Hansbrough	2007–08

NCAA TOURNAMENT MOP

James Worthy	1981–82
Donald Williams	1992–93
Sean May	2004–05
Wayne Ellington	2008–09

ACC PLAYER OF THE YEAR

Lennie Rosenbluth	1956–57
Pete Brennan	1957–58
Lee Shaffer	1959–60
Billy Cunningham	1964–65
Larry Miller	1966–67
Larry Miller	1967–68
Mitch Kupchak	1975–76
Phil Ford	1977–78
Michael Jordan	1983–84
Antawn Jamison	1997–98
Joe Forte*	2000–01
Tyler Hansbrough	2007–08
Ty Lawson	2008–09

* Shared this honor with another player.

COACH OF THE YEAR

Frank McGuire	1956–57
Dean Smith	1976–77
Dean Smith	1978–79
Dean Smith	1981–82
Dean Smith	1992–93
Bill Guthridge	1997–98
Matt Doherty	2000–01
Roy Williams	2005–06

A pennant celebrating Carolina's 1993 national championship.

TAR HEELS ACHIEVEMENTS

ACHIEVEMENT	YEAR
National Champions*	1923–24
NCAA Finalists	1946–47
NCAA Champions	1956–57
NCAA Finalists	1967–68
NCAA Finalists	1976–77
NCAA Finalists	1980–81
NCAA Champions	1981–82
NCAA Champions	1992–93
NCAA Champions	2004–05
NCAA Champions	2008–09

• *Awarded by the Helms Foundation.*

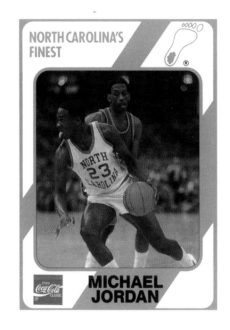

NORTH CAROLINA'S FINEST

MICHAEL JORDAN

RIGHT: Michael Jordan, the most exciting Tar Heel in school history.
BELOW: A team photo of the 1957 champs, signed by Lennie Rosenbluth.

The ACC

T he University of North Carolina is a member of the Atlantic Coast Conference, which started in 1953. In 2004, the ACC grew to 12 teams. These are the Tar Heels' neighbors …

THE ACC

1   Boston College Eagles
Chestnut Hill, Massachusetts

2   Clemson University Tigers
Clemson, South Carolina

3   Duke University Blue Devils
Durham, North Carolina

4   Florida State University Seminoles
Tallahassee, Florida

5   Georgia Tech Yellow Jackets
Atlanta, Georgia

6   University of Maryland Terrapins
College Park, Maryland

7   University of Miami Hurricanes
Coral Gables, Florida

8   University of North Carolina Tar Heels
Chapel Hill, North Carolina

9   North Carolina State University Wolfpack
Raleigh, North Carolina

10   University of Virginia Cavaliers
Charlottesville, Virginia

11   Virginia Tech Hokies
Blacksburg, Virginia

12   Wake Forest University Demon Deacons
Winston–Salem, North Carolina

The College Game

Collcge basketball may look like the same game you see professional teams play, but there are some important differences. The first is that college teams play half as many games as the pros do. That's because the players have to attend classes, write papers, and study for exams! Below are several other differences between college and pro basketball.

CLASS NOTES

Most college players are younger than pro players. They are student-athletes who have graduated from high school and now play on their school's varsity team, which is the highest level of competition. Most are between the ages of 18 and 22.

College players are allowed to compete for four seasons. Each year is given a different name or "class"—freshman (first year), sophomore (second year), junior (third year), and senior (fourth year). Sometimes highly skilled players leave college before graduation to play in the pros.

RULE BOOK

There are several differences between the rules in college basketball and the NBA. Here are the most important ones: 1) In college, games last 40 minutes. Teams play two 20-minute halves. In the pros, teams play 48-minute games, divided into four 12-minute quarters. 2) In college, players are disqualified after five personal fouls. In the pros, that number is six. 3) In college, the 3-point line is 20′ 9″ from the basket. In the pros, the line is three feet farther away.

WHO'S NUMBER 1?

How is the national championship of basketball decided? At the end of each season, the top teams are invited to play in the NCAA Tournament. The teams are divided into four groups, and the winner of each group advances to the Final Four. The Final Four consists of two semifinal games. The winners then play for the championship of college basketball.

CONFERENCE CALL

College basketball teams are members of athletic conferences. Each conference represents a different part of the country. For example, the Atlantic Coast Conference is made up of teams from up and down the East Coast. Teams that belong to the same conference usually play each other twice—once on each school's home court. Teams also play games outside their conference. Wins and losses in these games do not count in the conference standings. However, they are very important to a team's national ranking.

TOURNAMENT TIME

At the end of the year, most conferences hold a championship tournament. A team can have a poor record and still be invited to play in the NCAA Tournament if it wins the conference tournament. For many schools, this is an exciting "second chance." In most cases, the regular-season winner and conference tournament winner are given spots in the national tournament. The rest of the tournament "bids" are given to the best remaining teams.

Glossary

BASKETBALL WORDS TO KNOW

3-POINTERS—Baskets made from behind the 3-point line.

ALL-ACC—An honor given each year to the conference's best players at each position.

ALL-AMERICAN—A college player voted as the best at his position.

ASSISTS—Passes that lead to successful shots.

ATLANTIC COAST CONFERENCE (ACC)—A conference for teams in the southern part of the East Coast and Massachusetts. The ACC began play in 1953.

DIVISION I—The highest level of competition in college sports.

DRAFT—The annual meeting during which NBA teams choose from a group of the best college players. The draft is held each summer.

FAST BREAK—An offensive play in which the team with the ball rushes down the court to take a shot.

FINAL FOUR—The term for the last four teams remaining in the NCAA Tournament.

FOUR CORNERS OFFENSE—A strategy in which players spread out in the shape of a square and make safe, short passes hoping to run out the clock. UNC used the Four Corners in the days before the shot clock.

FULL-COURT PRESS—A defensive game plan in which a team pressures the opponent for the entire length of the court.

LINEUP—The list of players who are playing in a game.

LOOSE BALLS—Balls that are not controlled by either team.

MOST OUTSTANDING PLAYER (MOP)—The award given each year to the best player in the NCAA Tournament.

MOST VALUABLE PLAYER (MVP)—The award given each year to a team's best player; also given to the best player in a conference or tournament.

NATIONAL BASKETBALL ASSOCIATION (NBA)—The league that has been operating since 1946–47.

NATIONAL COLLEGIATE ATHLETIC ASSOCIATION (NCAA)—The organization that oversees the majority of college sports.

NCAA TOURNAMENT—The competition that determines the champion of college basketball.

OVERTIMES—The extra periods played when a game is tied after 48 minutes and then again after each extra period that ends in a tie.

PROFESSIONAL—A player or team that plays a sport for money. College players are not paid, so they are considered amateurs.

RECRUITED—Competed for a student-athlete. Each year colleges recruit the best high school players and offer them athletic scholarships.

SHOT CLOCK—The clock that keeps track of the amount of time that each team is allowed to have the ball. In college, a team must attempt a shot within 35 seconds.

SOUTHERN CONFERENCE—A conference for teams that play in the southern part of the country. It began play in 1921.

STANDINGS—A daily list of teams, starting with the team with the best record and ending with the team with the worst record.

TEAM BASKETBALL—A style of play that involves everyone on the court instead of just one or two stars.

TURNOVER—A play in which the team on offense loses possession of the ball.

ZONE DEFENSE—A defense in which players are responsible for guarding an area of the court rather than covering a specific offensive player.

OTHER WORDS TO KNOW

AGILE—Quick and graceful.

CAMPUS—The grounds and buildings of a college.

CENTURY—A period of 100 years.

COMPETITOR—Someone who has a strong desire to win.

DOMINATING—Completely controlling.

ELITE—Best.

FUNDAMENTALS—The most basic parts of something.

LOGO—A symbol or design that represents a company or team.

MASCOT—An animal or person believed to bring a group good luck.

OLYMPIC—Describing the international sports competition held every four years.

RIVALRIES—Extremely emotional competitions.

SATIN—A smooth, shiny fabric.

STRATEGY—A plan or method for succeeding.

SYNTHETIC—Made in a laboratory, not in nature.

TRADITION—A belief or custom that is handed down from generation to generation.

UNFORGETTABLE—Amazing.

Places to Go

ON THE ROAD

NORTH CAROLINA TAR HEELS
300 Skipper Bowles Drive
Chapel Hill, North Carolina 27514
(919) 962–6000

NAISMITH MEMORIAL BASKETBALL HALL OF FAME
1000 West Columbus Avenue
Springfield, Massachusetts 01105
(877) 4HOOPLA

ON THE WEB

THE NORTH CAROLINA TAR HEELS   tarheelblue.cstv.com
  • *Learn more about the Tar Heels*

ATLANTIC COAST CONFERENCE   www.theacc.com
  • *Learn more about the ACC Conference teams*

THE BASKETBALL HALL OF FAME   www.hoophall.com
  • *Learn more about history's greatest players*

ON THE BOOKSHELF

To learn more about the sport of basketball, look for these books at your library or bookstore:
  • Labrecque, Ellen. *Basketball.* Ann Arbor, Michigan: Cherry Lake Publishing, 2009.
  • Porterfield, Jason. *Basketball in the ACC.* New York, New York: Rosen Central, 2008.
  • Stewart, Mark and Kennedy, Mike. *Swish: the Quest for Basketball's Perfect Shot.* Minneapolis, Minnesota: Millbrook Press, 2009.

Index

PAGE NUMBERS IN **BOLD** REFER TO ILLUSTRATIONS.

About the Author

MARK STEWART has written more than 30 books on basketball players and teams, and over 100 sports books for kids. He has also interviewed dozens of athletes, politicians, and celebrities. Although Mark grew up in New York, he became curious about UNC basketball in the 1970s while watching American Basketball Association games on TV. Ex-Tar Heels Larry Brown, Larry Miller, Charlie Scott, Billy Cunningham, and Bobby Jones were ABA All-Stars. Mark comes from a family of writers. His grandfather was Sunday Editor of *The New York Times* and his mother was Articles Editor for *Ladies' Home Journal* and *McCall's*. Mark became interested in sports during lazy summer days spent at the Connecticut home of his father's godfather, sportswriter John R. Tunis. Mark is a graduate of Duke University, with a degree in History. He still likes the Tar Heels but roots for the Blue Devils when the two teams play. He lives with his wife Sarah, and daughters Mariah and Rachel, overlooking Sandy Hook, New Jersey.

MATT ZEYSING is the resident historian at the Basketball Hall of Fame in Springfield, Massachusetts. His research interests include the origins of the game of basketball, the development of professional basketball in the first half of the 20th century, and the culture and meaning of basketball in American society.

mL

11/10